THIS JOURNAL BELONGS TO:
AF417882
DAD
SON
Name:
Name:
We start this journey with:

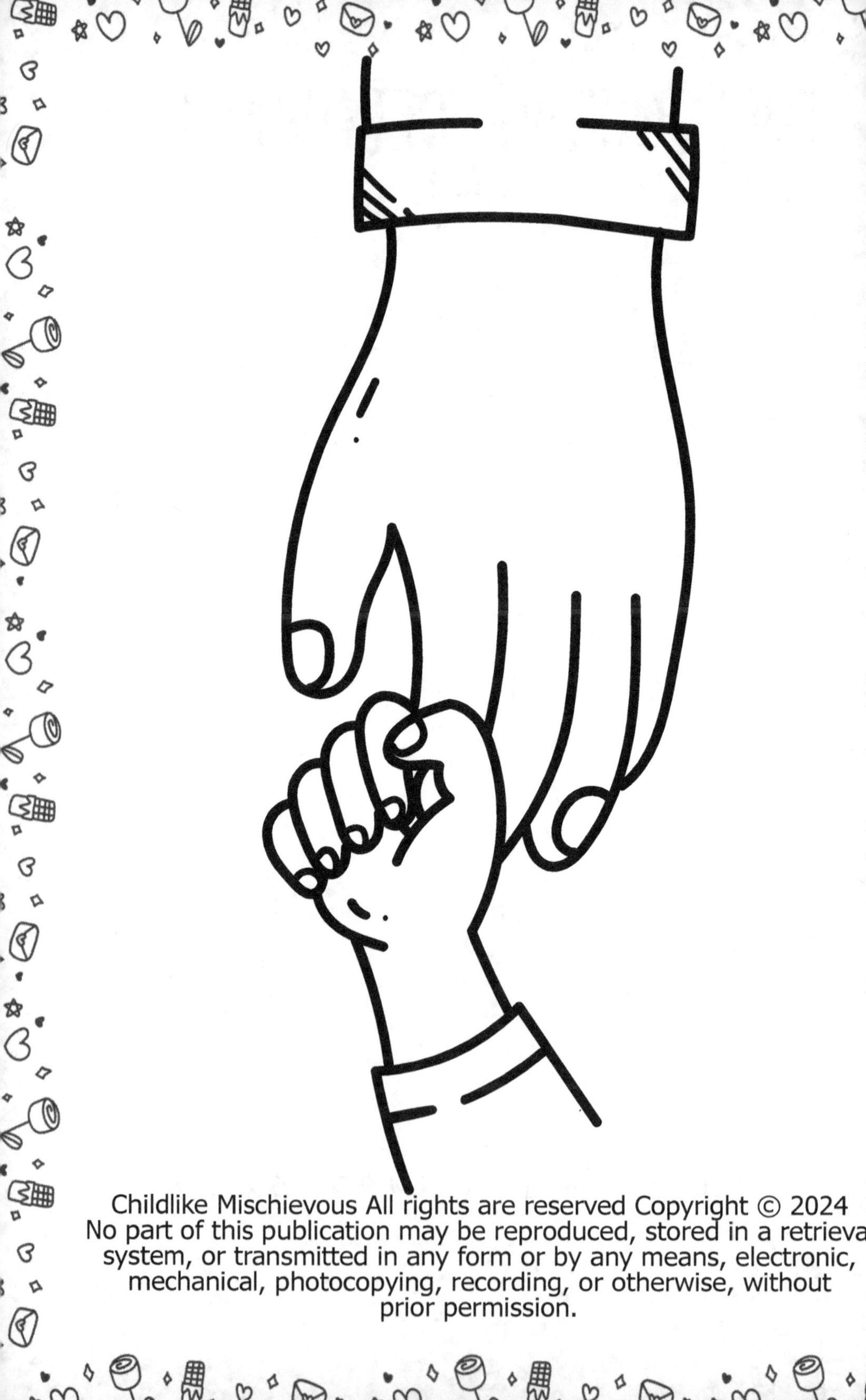

Today marks the beginning of a special journey together - a journey of discovery, connection, and meaningful conversations through this journal. This is more than just a place for words; it's a space where you can share your thoughts, dreams, and moments that bring you closer as father and son. As you fill these pages, remember that every entry is a step toward understanding each other more deeply and creating memories that will last a lifetime. Here's to the start of something truly amazing - your shared story.

About Dad

Name: _______________________________

Age: _______________________________

Hair Color: _______________________________

Eye Color: _______________________________

Height: _______________________________

Favorite Color: _______________________________

Favorite Animal: _______________________________

A list of names my Son uses for me:

____

____

____

About Dad

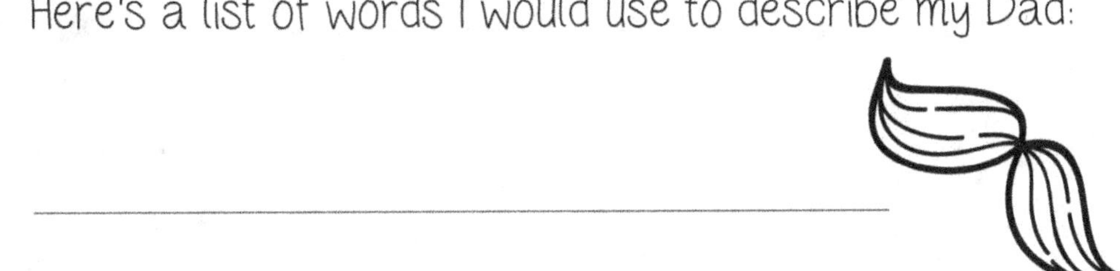

Here's a list of words I would use to describe my Dad:

____

____

____

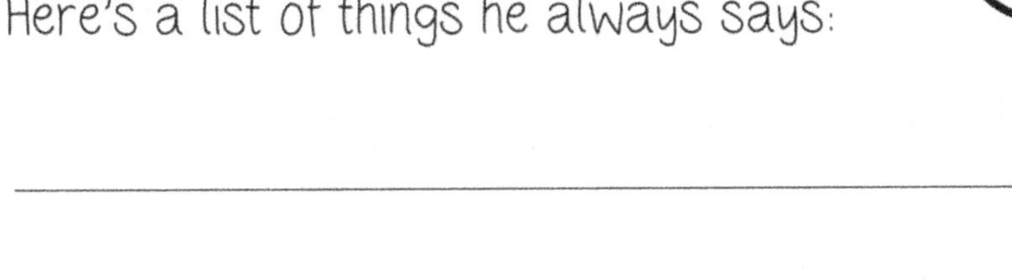

Here's a list of things he always says:

____

____

____

____

About Me

Name: ____________________________

Age: ____________________________

Hair Color: ____________________________

Eye Color: ____________________________

Height: ____________________________

Favorite Color: ____________________________

Favorite Animal: ____________________________

A list of names Dad uses for me:

____

____

____

About Me

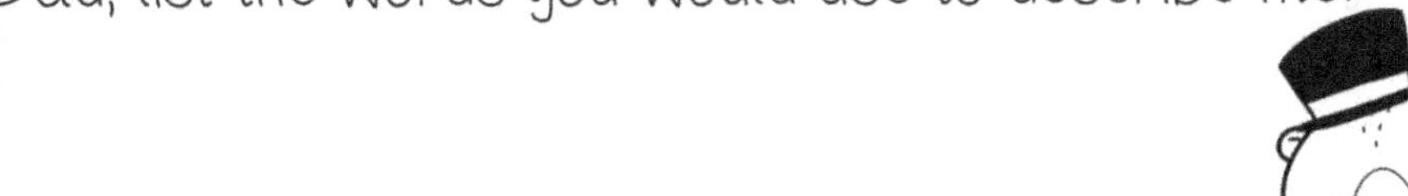

Dad, list the words you would use to describe me:

____

____

____

____

List the things I say all the time:

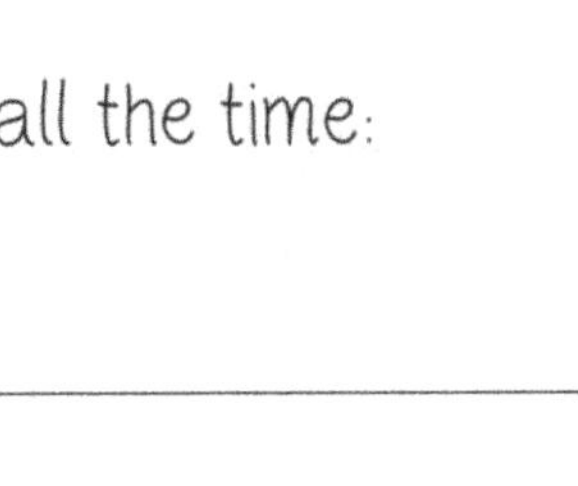
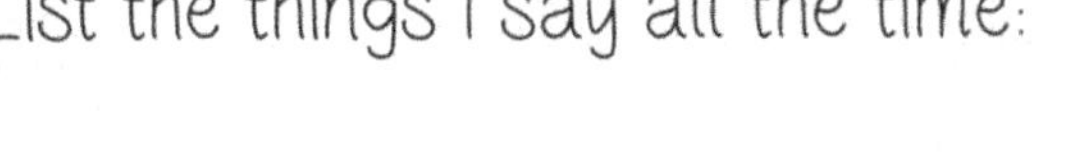
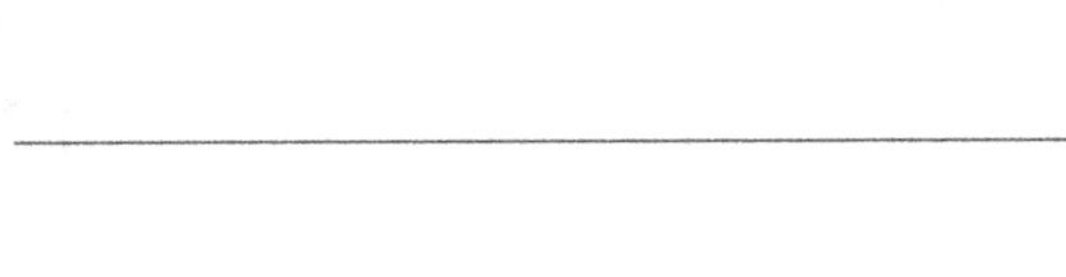
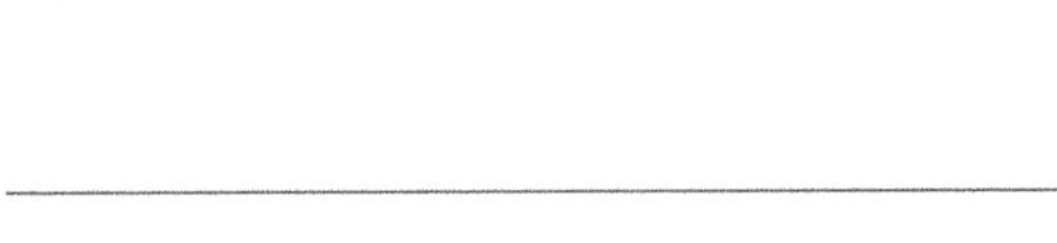
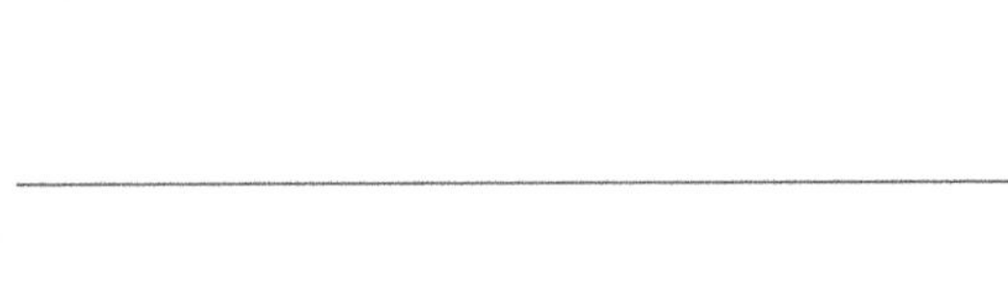
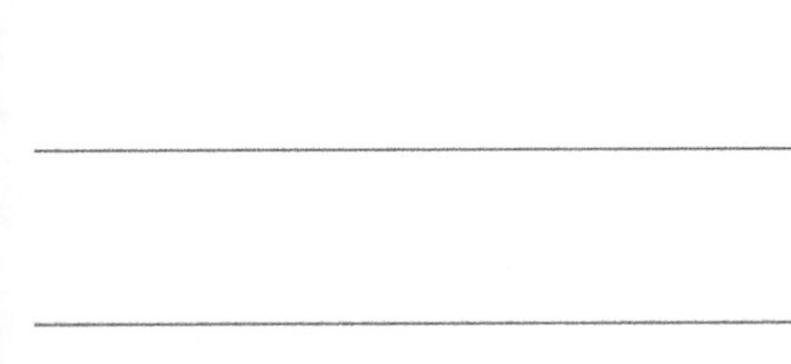

____

____

____

____

Dad and Me

Dad and Me

Here is a silly song we wrote:

Dad

Son, these are the ways I think we are similar...

____

____

____

____

____

These are the things I think are different about us...

____

____

____

____

____

Son

Dad, these are the ways I think we are similar...

These are the things I think are different about us...

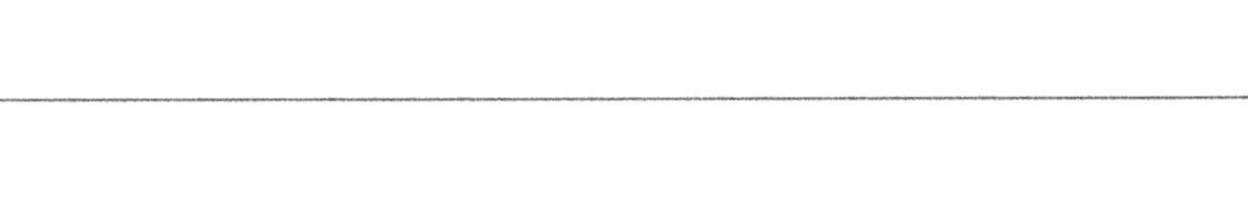

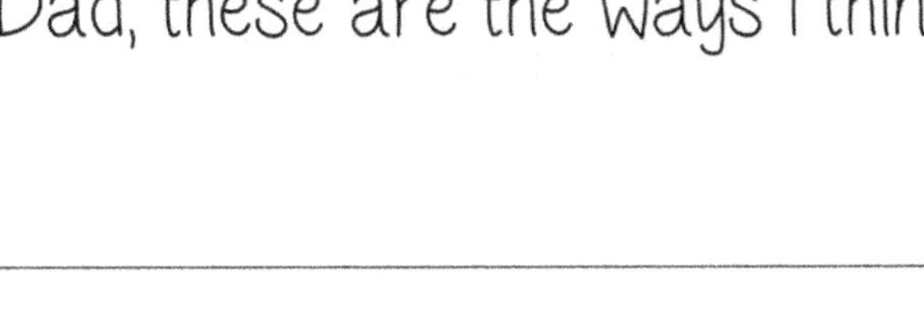
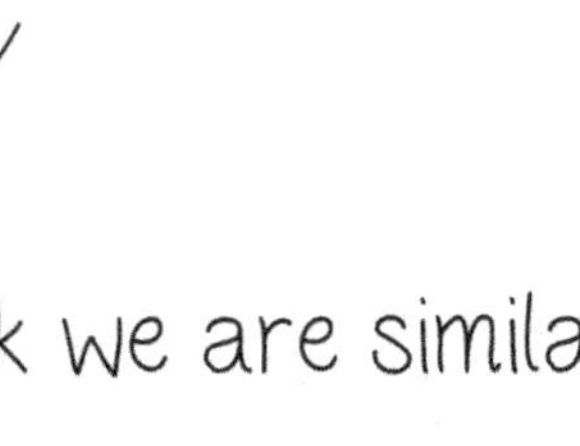

Dad

The time and place I was born is...

My most memorable birthday is...

My favorite ever present was...

Son

The time and place I was born is...

____

____

My most memorable birthday is...

____

____

My favorite ever present was...

____

____

Dad

Son, you are strong and kind, inside and out, because

1

2

3

Son

Dad, you are strong and kind, inside and out, because...

1

2

3

Dad

My very first memory is...

____
____
____
____

My first memory of school is...

____
____
____
____

Son

My very first memory is...

____

____

____

____

My first memory of school is...

____

____

____

Dad

Son, this is what I admire about you and why...

I've always wanted to tell you...

Son

Dad, this is what I admire about you and why...

I've always wanted to tell you...

Dad

When I was young I wanted to be...

____

____

____

____

When I was young, a goal I had for when I grew up was...

____

____

____

____

Son

When I grow up I want to be...

____

____

____

____

A goal I have for when I grow up is...

____

____

____

____

Dad

My favorite place to go when I was young was...

____

____

____

____

If I could go anywhere now, it would be...

____

____

____

____

Son

My favorite place to go is...

____

____

____

____

If I could go anywhere, it would it be...

____

____

____

____

Dad

Some interesting facts about our family are...

My fondest memories of our family are...

Son

The things I like best about our family are...

My fondest memories of our family are...

Dad

Some things I'd like to do with family time are...

____

____

____

____

Some things I wish were different are...

____

____

____

____

Son

Some things I'd like to do with family time are...

Some things I wish were different are...

Family Photos

Family Photos

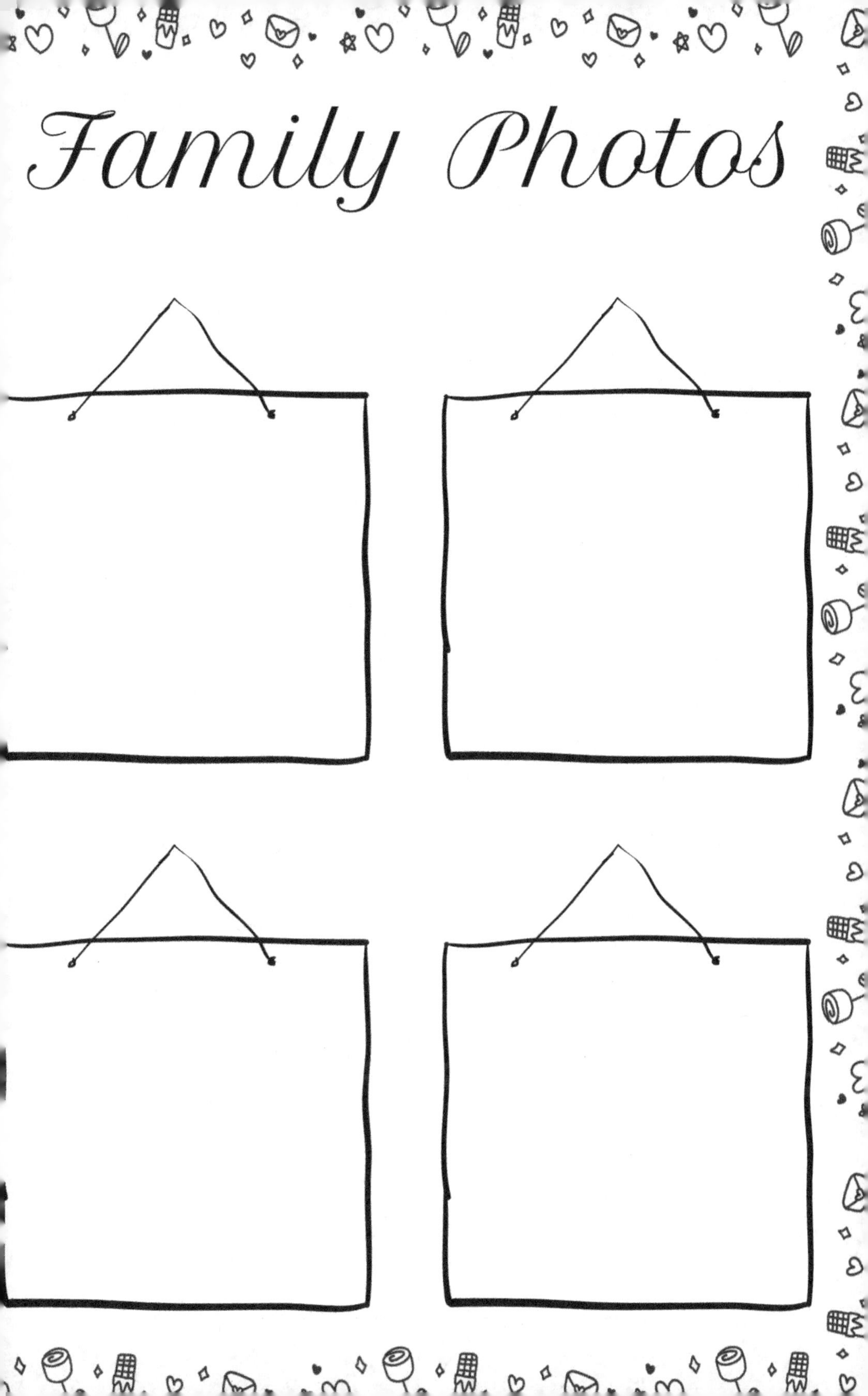

Dad

Something that makes me feel happy is...

____

____

____

____

____

Something that would make me happy in the future is...

____

____

____

____

Son

Something that makes me feel happy is...

Something that would make me happy in the future is...

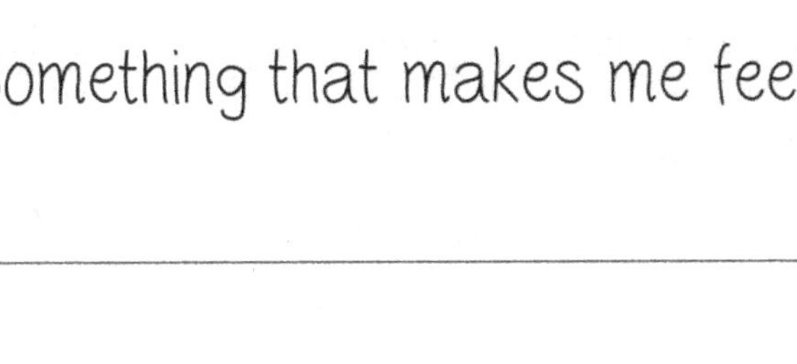
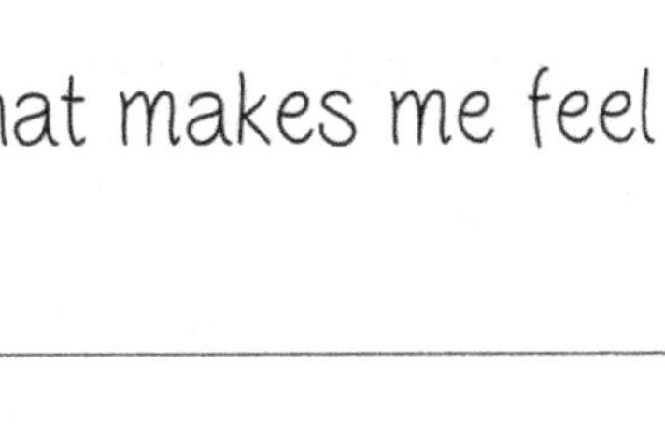
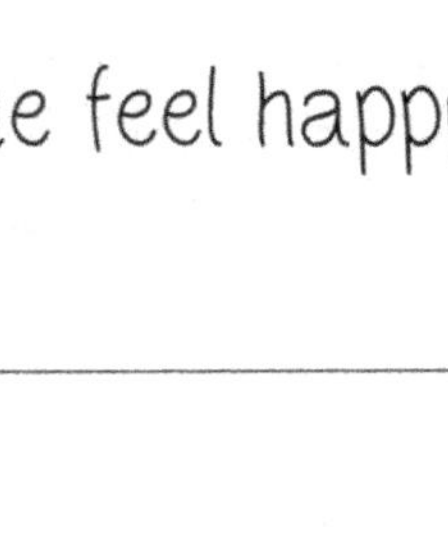

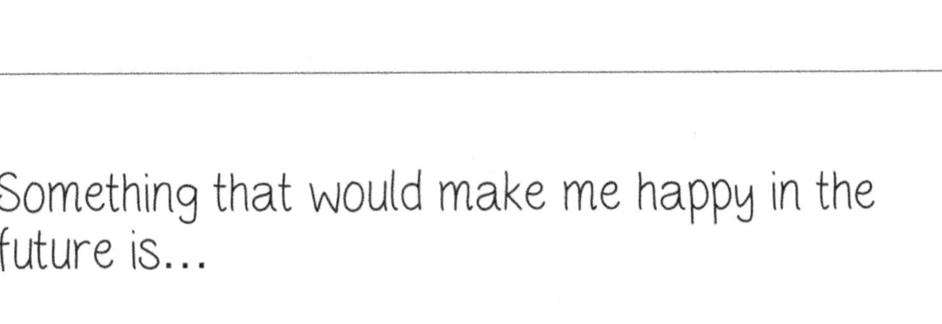
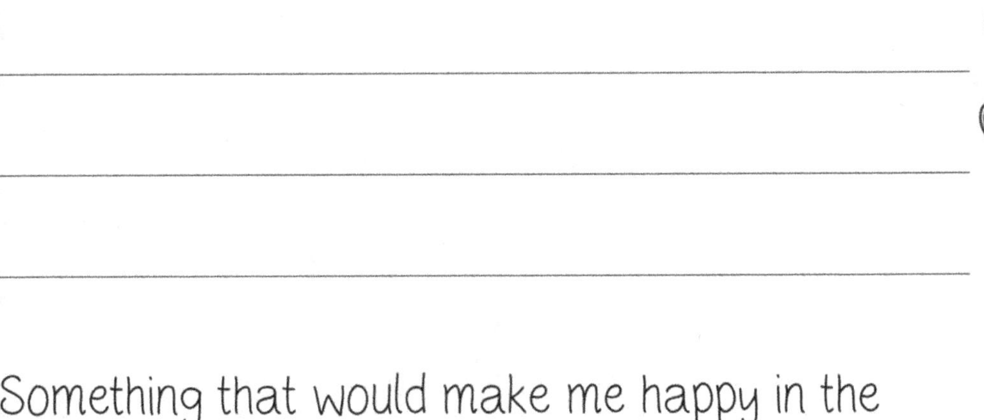
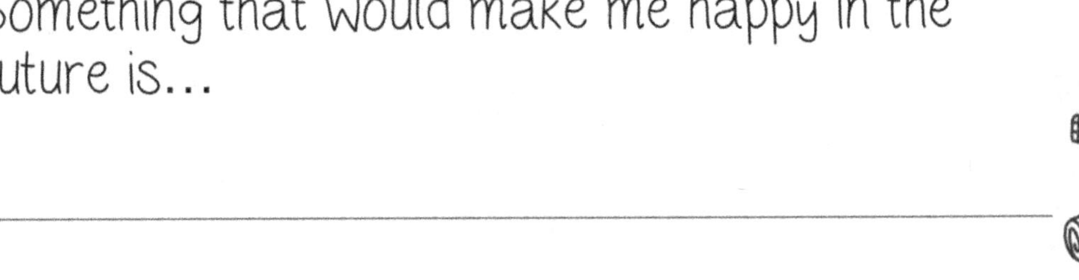

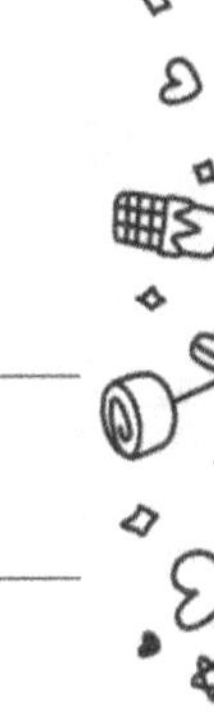

Dad
Son, something you do that makes me smile is...

Son

Dad, something you do that makes me smile is...

Dad

If I could have three wishes, they would be...

1

2

3

Son

If I could have three wishes, they would be...

1

2

3

Dad

Something that makes me feel sad is...

____

____

____

____

Something I can do to help me handle this is...

____

____

____

Son

Something that makes me feel sad is...

____

____

____

____

Something I can do to help me handle this is...

____

____

____

____

Dad

Son, these are your three most amazing qualities...

1

2

3

Son

Dad, these are your three most amazing qualities...

1

2

3

Dad

If I could imagine myself wearing an amazing outfit that would make me feel more confident when I'm anxious, it would look like this...

Son

Son... When you feel anxious or lack confidence, imagine yourself wearing an amazing outfit. Everyone thinks you look wonderful.
Draw a picture and describe what it looks like...

____

____

Dad

What I was like as a child...

How I am different now...

Son

If I become a Dad when I grow up, I'd like to be...

____

____

____

____

The names I'd choose for my children are...

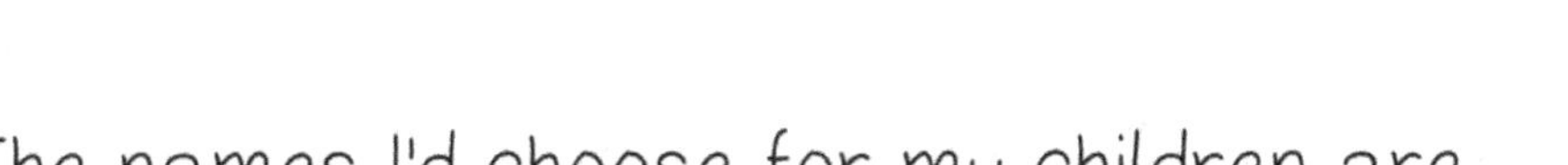

____

____

____

____

Dad

Dad, tell me about the weirdest dream you've ever had.

Son

Son, tell me about the weirdest dream you've ever had...

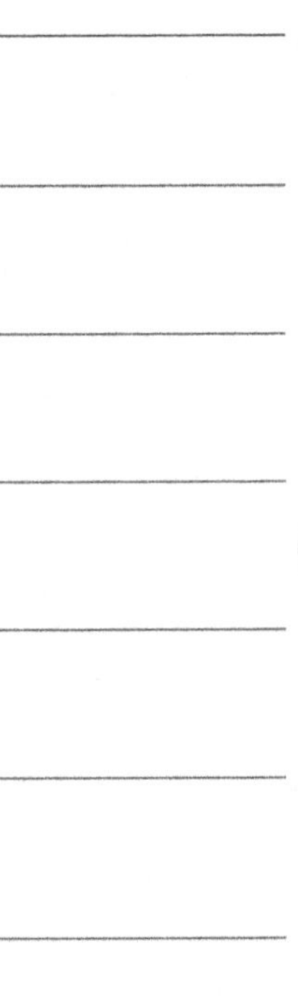

Dad

Something that makes me feel mad is...

____

____

____

____

Something I can do to help me handle this is...

____

____

____

Son

Something that makes me feel mad is...

____

____

____

____

Something I can do to help me handle this is…

____

____

____

Dad

Son

Dad

Son, because of you I learned...

____

____

____

____

____

You were right about...

____

____

____

____

Son

Dad, because of you I learned...

____

____

____

____

You were right about...

____

____

____

____

Dad

If I could have three superpowers, they would be...

1

2

3

Son

If I could have three superpowers, they would be...

1.

2.

3.

Dad

My best friends as a child were...

____

____

____

My best friends now are...

____

____

____

What I've learned about friendships are...

____

____

____

Son

My best friends are...

____

____

____

The things I like best about my friends are...

____

____

____

The things I don't like about my friends are...

____

____

____

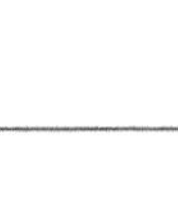

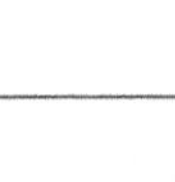

Dad

Dad, did you sleep with a cuddly toy when you were young?
Tell me about it?

Son

My favorite cuddly toy is a __________ called __________.
I will never throw it away because...

Dad

Something that makes me feel anxious is...

Something I can do to help me handle this is...

Son

Something that makes me feel anxious is...

____

____

____

____

Something I can do to help me handle this is...

____

____

____

____

Dad

Tunes

My top 10 songs of all time are...

1. ______________________________
2. ______________________________
3. ______________________________
4. ______________________________
5. ______________________________
6. ______________________________
7. ______________________________
8. ______________________________
9. ______________________________
10. ______________________________

Son

My favourite top 10 songs are...

Dad

My favourite hobbies when I was young were...

____

____

____

Something I would like to try is...

____

____

____

I would like to do this by...

____

____

____

Son

My favourite hobbies are...

___

___

___

Something I would like to try is...

___

___

___

I would like to do this by...

___

___

___

Dad

Dad, tell me about a kind thing you did for someone...

Son

Son, tell me about a kind thing you did for someone...

Dad

Son, thank you for always...

Thank you for showing me...

Son

Dad, thank you for always...

____

____

____

____

Thank you for showing me...

____

____

____

____

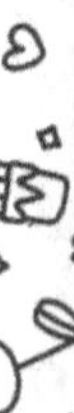

Dad

This is the story of the most embarrassing thing that happened to me when I was young...

____

____

____

____

____

____

____

____

____

Son

This is the story of my most embarrassing moment…

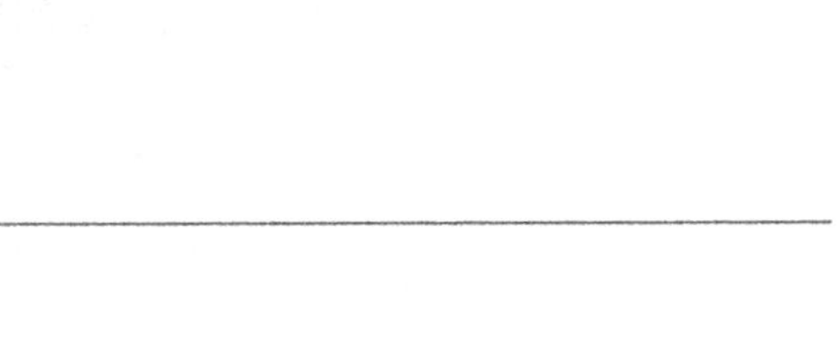

Dad

The person I used to go to with my worries
when I was Young was...

____

____

____

____

If I ever want to talk about my feelings, I solemnly
swear to speak to you or ...

____

____

____

Signature: _____________________________

Son

The person I will go to with my worries will be...

____

____

____

____

If I ever want to talk about my feelings, I solemnly swear that I will talk to you or...

____

____

____

____

Signature: _______________________________

Dad
Other Things I Want To Say To You,

Son

Other Things I Want To Say To You,

Dad

Other Things I Want To Say To You,

Son

Other Things I Want To Say To You,

Use these additional pages if you need more space for your answer.

Congratulations to both of you on completing this journal! This is a special accomplishment, showing the strong connection and love that you share. Every page is filled with memories, laughter, and important conversations that have brought you closer. As you move forward, always remember that this journal is just the beginning of your journey together. No matter what challenges or adventures come your way, your bond is unbreakable. Keep building memories, supporting each other, and creating moments that will last a lifetime. Here's to the incredible relationship you have and all the wonderful times still ahead!